W9-AOL-795

MYTHS FROM AROUND THE WORLD

ANCIENT ROMAN MYTHS

By Brian Innes

Gareth Stevens
Publishing

Please visit our Web site www.garethstevens.com. For a free color catalog of all our high-quality books, call toll free 1-800-542-2595 or fax 1-877-542-2596.

Library of Congress Cataloging-in-Publication Data
Innes, Brian.
     Ancient Roman myths / Brian Innes.
          p. cm. — (Myths from around the world)
     Includes index.
     ISBN 978-1-4339-3527-5 (library binding) — ISBN 978-1-4339-3528-2 (pbk.)
     ISBN 978-1-4339-3529-9 (6-pack)
     1. Mythology, Roman—Juvenile literature. 2. Gods, Roman—Juvenile literature.
     3. Rome—Religious life and customs—Juvenile literature. I. Title.
BL803.I66 2010
398.20937—dc22   2009037158

Published in 2010 by
Gareth Stevens Publishing
111 East 14th Street, Suite 349
New York, NY 10003

© 2010 The Brown Reference Group Ltd.

For Gareth Stevens Publishing:
Art Direction: Haley Harasymiw
Editorial Direction: Kerri O'Donnell

For The Brown Reference Group Ltd:
Editorial Director: Lindsey Lowe
Managing Editor: Tim Cooke
Editor: Henry Russell
Children's Publisher: Anne O'Daly
Picture Manager: Sophie Mortimer
Design Manager: David Poole
Designers: Tim Mayer and John Walker
Production Director: Alastair Gourlay

Picture Credits:
Front Cover: Shutterstock: br; Lawrence Gough b; Javarman t

Corbis: Roger Wood 41; iStock: 7; James Group Studios 23; Jupiter Images: Liquidlibrary 21t; Photos.com 10, 13t, 16, 17b, 28/29, 29t, 33b; Stockxpert 17t, 24, 25r, 32, 40, 43; Shutterstock: 15, 20; Murat Besler 36; Tony Carr 39; Clara 33t, 37; Bertrand Collet 21b; Frog-traveller 5; Fabrizio Gattuso 13b; Vladimir Khirman 35, 43; Stanislav Khrapov 11; Mikhail Khromov 31; Kevin H. Knuth 9b; Denis Kornilov 19; Lagui 29b; Ligak 12; Oorka 25l; Pseudolongino 27; ukrphoto 9t; Witchcraft 44; Claudio Zaccherini 8

Publisher's note to educators and parents: Our editors have carefully reviewed the Web sites that appear on p. 47 to ensure that they are suitable for students. Many Web sites change frequently, however, and we cannot guarantee that a site's future contents will continue to meet our high standards of quality and educational value. Be advised that students should be closely supervised whenever they access the Internet.

Manufactured in the United States of America
1 2 3 4 5 6 7 8 9   12 11 10

CPSIA compliance information: Batch #BRW0102GS: For further information contact Gareth Stevens, New York, New York at 1-800-542-2595.

Contents

Introduction

Myths are mirrors of humanity. They reflect the soul of a culture and try to give profound answers in a seemingly mysterious world. They give the people an understanding of their place in the world and the universe.

Found in all civilizations, myths sometimes combine fact and fiction and at other times are complete fantasy.

Every culture has its own myth. Yet, globally, there are common themes, even across civilizations that had no contact with each other. The most common myths deal with the creation of the world or of a particular site, like a mountain or a lake. Other myths deal with the origin of humans or describe the heroes and gods who either made the world inhabitable or who provided humans with something essential, such as the ancient Greek Titan Prometheus, who gave fire, and the Native American Wunzh, who was given divine instructions on cultivating corn. There are also myths about the end of the world, death, and the afterlife.

The origin of evil and death are also common themes. Examples of such myths are the Biblical Eve eating the forbidden fruit and the ancient Greek story of Pandora opening the sealed box.

Additionally, there are flood myths, myths about the sun and the moon, and myths of peaceful places of reward, such as heaven or Elysium, and of places of punishment, such as hell or Tartarus. Myths also teach human values, such as courage and honesty.

This book deals with some of the most important myths of ancient Rome. Following each myth is an explanation of how the myth related to the real life in the Roman world. A glossary at the end of the book identifies the major mythological and historical characters and explains many cultural terms.

Ancient Roman Mythology

The mythologies of most cultures are a mix of newly created stories and myths adapted from neighboring or more ancient cultures. Many of the most popular Roman myths are based on ancient Greek myths, which were adapted to enhance the importance of Rome.

The early Romans imagined their gods as formless powers without personalities but with strong links to particular places. They associated Jupiter, the sky god, with oak groves and the tops of hills, and they dedicated patches of ground struck by lightning to him. The goddess Vesta ruled the hearth, the heart of the home.

When the Romans came into contact with Greek culture, in the sixth century B.C., they were so impressed that they began to imagine their own gods in human form, like the Greek gods, and to build temples in their honor.

By the first century B.C., the Romans had adopted Apollo as their own and given other Greek gods Roman names and new identities. In his epic poem the *Aeneid*, Virgil (70–19 B.C.) changed Zeus and his wife, Hera, from the marginal figures depicted by the Greek writer Homer into the imposing deities of Jupiter and Juno.

The Romans also adapted Greek myths to link them directly with Rome. According to the Roman historian Livy (59 B.C.–A.D. 17), Hercules—the Greek hero Heracles—once stopped off where Rome was later built to slay a monster that was terrorizing the people.

Not even the most important original Roman myth, the founding of Rome by Romulus, escaped Greek influence. In the third century B.C., a story that the hero of Troy, Prince Aeneas, was involved in the founding of Rome became popular. Trouble was, Aeneas was supposed to have lived some 400 years before Romulus. So, in the *Aeneid*, Virgil made Aeneas an ancestor of Romulus, thereby allowing the Romans to celebrate both their mythical Trojan origins and their legendary founder Romulus.

Homer was a Greek poet of the ninth or the eighth century B.C. whose works greatly influenced Roman literature.

5

Romulus and Remus

According to legend, Rome was founded by Romulus, who was raised with his twin brother Remus by a she-wolf. The two boys later fought over who should rule the new settlement.

Legend has it that when the Greeks burned and destroyed the city of Troy in Asia Minor (roughly present-day Turkey) more than 3,000 years ago, Prince Aeneas of Troy, the son of the goddess of love, Venus (Aphrodite to the Greeks), escaped the flames and sailed to the west. He and his companions eventually arrived in Italy, on a plain called Latium. The ruler there, Latinus, had foreseen their coming in his dreams and been told that the marriage of his daughter Lavinia to Aeneas would be the beginning of a great and powerful people. The wedding went ahead, and in due course Aeneas's son Ascanius founded the town of Alba Longa.

One of Ascanius's descendants was Procas, who had two sons, Numitor and Amulius. Numitor was the older of the boys and so was the rightful heir, but Amulius drove his older brother into exile and claimed the throne for himself. To be sure that there would be no one to succeed Numitor, Amulius then made Numitor's only child, Rhea Silvia, a Vestal Virgin. A Vestal Virgin was a priestess of the temple of the hearth goddess Vesta (Hestia), and Amulius's decree meant that Rhea Silvia could never marry or have any children. However, the god Mars (Ares) visited Rhea Silvia secretly, and soon after she gave birth to twin sons. Amulius was furious that she had ignored her obligations. He drowned her in the Tiber River, then threw her babies in a basket into the river.

Animal Rescue

The basket eventually drifted ashore by a fig tree in the shallows at the foot of a hill called the Palatine. The cries of the two babies attracted a she-wolf. The animal saved the twins' lives by suckling them in a cave. Some time later a herdsman called Faustulus found the twins in the woods, took them home to his wife, and brought them up as his own, naming them Romulus and Remus.

According to legend, Romulus and Remus were suckled by a she-wolf after they had been thrown into the Tiber River.

The two boys grew up to be strong young men. One day they quarreled with some shepherds, who captured Remus and took him to their master, who was none other than the exiled Numitor. Romulus followed the shepherds and pleaded with Numitor to release his brother. Numitor realized that the twins were actually his long-lost grandsons.

With the help of Romulus and Remus, Numitor then killed Amulius and recovered Alba Longa. The twins decided to build a town of their own, choosing the site where they had been washed ashore in the basket. Which of them was to be the new town's ruler? To answer this question, Romulus climbed to the top of the Palatine Hill, Remus to the top of the nearby Aventine Hill, and both waited for a sign from the gods. The sign came soon enough. Six vultures circled over the Aventine, but twelve appeared above the Palatine. Romulus declared that he was to rule the new town.

While Remus looked on jealously, Romulus began to build the new town on the Palatine. Finally, Remus could stand it no more and contemptuously showed how easy it was to jump over the half-built walls. Angered, Romulus challenged Remus to a fight and killed him with his sword. Romulus was duly crowned king, and the new town was named in his honor. Centuries later, the Romans placed these events at 753 B.C. and calculated their calendar from this date.

The Founding of Rome

No one knows if Romulus, the legendary founder of Rome, ever actually existed, but there is no doubt that the settlement eventually became the base for a powerful and long-lasting civilization.

The story of Romulus and Remus being suckled by a she-wolf is almost certainly a myth, but it was a very popular one. The wolf appears on early Roman coins. Many experts think that the famous bronze sculpture of a she-wolf in a museum in Rome is Etruscan in origin—and it was the Etruscans who ruled Rome for the city's first 250 years.

By 700 B.C., the Greeks dominated the eastern half of the Mediterranean but their influence extended only as far as the southern tip of Italy. The main powers of the western Mediterranean were the Carthaginians, who were based in North Africa, and the Etruscans, who lived in northwestern Italy. They were fierce trading rivals.

Meanwhile, tribes of peasant farmers began to move from central Europe across the Alps and into Italy. After several centuries a group of them settled on the southern side of the Tiber River, on the plain of Latium. These people, known as the Latins, founded the town of Alba Longa, which became the birthplace of the Roman empire.

This metal sculpture of a two-horse chariot and a charioteer was made by the early Etruscans.

The Etruscans and the Latins bought and sold each other's goods at a trading post on the Tiber River that was guarded on the Latin side by a strong fort on top of the Palatine Hill. On the six surrounding hills were small villages. In between, on low marshy ground, lay an open-air market—known as the Forum—and a cemetery.

This Roman mosaic reflects the importance of farming to the early members of this great civilization.

Rise of the Roman Republic

Around 750 B.C. an Etruscan chieftain crossed the Tiber and destroyed Alba Longa. A new settlement—Rome—arose on the hills around the Forum. For the next 250 years, Etruscan kings ruled over the Latins. The Etruscans brought "civilization"—which means "city living"—to the farmers. They built a temple to the god Jupiter on the hill called the Capitol.

Around 500 B.C., the people of Rome drove the Etruscans out of their city. They then decided that, instead of being ruled by a king, they would elect two consuls, or magistrates, each year to head their government. This was the start of the great Roman republic, which lasted until Augustus became the first emperor of Rome in 27 B.C.

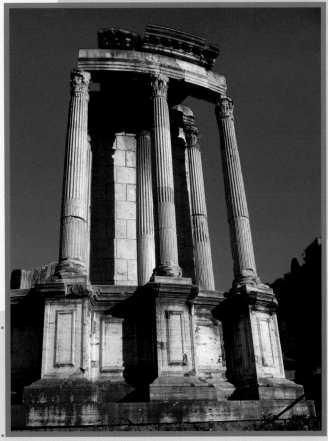

As Rome became the heart of a great empire, huge monuments were built throughout the city.

Diana and Actaeon

The gods forbade mere mortals to look at them without permission, so when the hunter Actaeon saw the goddess Diana bathing in a pool she took terrible revenge on him.

Diana (Artemis to the Greeks), the goddess of fertility and hunting, was the daughter of the king of the gods, Jupiter (Zeus), and Latona (Leto), and the twin sister of Apollo. When she was a child—perhaps as young as three—she asked her father to grant her eternal virginity.

Accompanied by nymphs, Diana roamed forests, mountains, and marshes, where she danced, hunted game with her silver arrows, and guarded young animals from hunters. She also protected girls and pregnant women, and Roman women prayed and made offerings to her in order to conceive and give birth safely. Like her brother, Diana could bring healing but she could also bring disease and death if she was angered. When a woman died in childbirth, people said that Diana had shot her down for offending the goddess in some way.

Diana fiercely protected her nymphs. Once, her father seduced one of them, Callisto, who then gave birth to a boy named Arcas. Diana punished Callisto by turning her into a bear, and when Arcas grew up he unknowingly hunted and killed his own mother.

Diana was equally protective of her own purity and gravely punished anyone who dishonored her. One man who offended her was a hunter called Actaeon. His unfortunate story began when he was out hunting in a forest one day with his

This is a statue of Artemis, the Greek precursor of the Roman Diana.

hair burst through his skin—Diana had turned him into a stag (a male deer). Seeing his own reflection in the pool, Actaeon fled in terror but his own hounds immediately gave chase—cheered on wildly by his followers, who did not realize that the stag was in fact their master.

followers and pack of hounds and saw Diana and her nymphs bathing in a pool. Furious, the goddess looked for her bow, but it was out of reach, so instead she splashed water in the hunter's face.

Instantly, a pair of branching horns sprouted from Actaeon's head, then his neck lengthened, his ears grew points, his hands and feet became hooves, and

Hounded to Death

Actaeon raced desperately through the trees, the baying hounds hot on his heels. He tried to cry out to his followers, "I am Actaeon! Recognize your master!" but he could not speak. The bloodthirsty pack of dogs soon caught him and ravenously tore him to pieces in front of his followers.

Religion in Ancient Rome

Like the Greeks, the Romans worshipped a host of gods, whom they believed controlled all aspects of human life—for better or worse, according to their pleasure or displeasure.

These figures, carved in relief on the wall of a temple, are thought to depict ancient Roman priests on their way to, or performing, a religious ceremony.

The Romans held festivals for each god, and they built hundreds of temples where they regularly sought favors, in everything from personal health to success in war, by praying and offering food, wine, and money. Many also had a *lararium*, or shrine, at home, where they prayed and made daily offerings to statuettes of *lares*, or household gods.

Inside each temple was a statue of its god in human form. Outside the building was an altar, where priests elected from the nobility often sacrificed animals and studied the viscera, or entrails, to determine the will of the god. The entrails were then burned on the altar, and the animals were cooked and eaten.

When Roman consuls and emperors faced big decisions, they tried to find out the will of the gods by telling their plans to

In the second century A.D., some Romans formed a religious cult that worshipped the Persian god Mithra.

special priests called augurs. The augurs then scattered grain in front of their chickens. If the birds ate the grain, the plan was good.

Diana Worship

The main temple of the goddess Diana was on the Aventine Hill in Rome. An even older place of Diana worship was outside the city, at Nemi on the shore of Lake Alban. Here, the priest, called the *rex silvae*, or king of the woods, had to be a runaway slave who had killed his predecessor in combat after breaking a bough from a sacred tree.

Many Romans later lost interest in their traditional gods and adopted "mystery" cults that offered secret rites and, often, a happy afterlife — something the old gods never did. The cult of the wine god Bacchus came from Greece (where he was called Dionysus). The cult of Jesus Christ came from Palestine. Although Christians were persecuted for years, in A.D. 380 Christianity became the Roman state religion.

Lake Alban was the focal point of the religious cult of the goddess Diana.

The God with Two Faces

A solely Roman god, Janus had two faces, joined back to back. They helped him to see into both the past and the future—and to seduce a beautiful but mischievous nymph.

Janus was the custodian of the universe, the guardian of gates and doors, and the god of all beginnings and endings. The Romans dedicated the first day of the year to him. He originated all important changes, such as the years and the seasons, planting, harvesting, birth, growing up, marriage, and changes of luck. Janus was also responsible for major changes, such as the shifts from primitive life to civilization, from country to town, and, most importantly to the Romans, from peace to war. Almost as powerful as Jupiter (Zeus to the Greeks), the king of the gods, Janus also controlled all things, and the world moved at his command, Romans said, "like a door on its hinges."

The Romans believed that Janus was originally a king, a son of Apollo, who left Greece to become the first king of Italy, founding a town called Janiculum by the Tiber River on the plain of Latium. Here he instituted the worship of the gods and the building of temples, and even became a god himself.

The Golden Age

When Jupiter banished his own father, Saturn (Cronus), from Mount Olympus, the home of the gods, Saturn took refuge with Janus, shared his kingship, and taught the Latins many skills, including how to farm. His reign with Janus was so popular and peaceful that it became known as the Golden Age.

Janus was one of the gods who guarded Rome. According to legend, he saved the city when the Sabines, a group of invaders from the north, attacked its gates. There was particularly fierce fighting at one gate, and it seemed as if the Sabine forces might gain entry and capture Rome. Janus opened a hot spring, flooding the gateway and driving the invaders back.

In religious ceremonies and before wars and other important ventures, Janus was always the first god that the Romans called on, because it was through him that prayers could reach the other gods. The Romans kept the gates of his great temple in Rome closed in peacetime and open at the outbreak of war. There were three short periods in Roman history when the gates remained closed.

Other temples of Janus had a door and three windows on each of their four sides, representing the seasons and the months. His statues in the temples had four faces. Elsewhere they had two: an old face, looking back, and a young one, looking ahead. He was also depicted holding a key in his left hand, for opening and closing all things, and a scepter in his right, for controlling all things.

Janus found his two faces useful when he fell in love with Carna, a nymph who lived on the Palatine Hill, the site where Rome was later built. Carna was a flirt who tricked her would-be lovers by leading them to a distant cave and then slipping away. Janus, however, could see her creeping away behind him and caught her. Soon after, he made her a goddess with the power to open and shut doors.

These ancient Roman coins depict the two-faced god Janus.

The Roman Calendar

Not only was Julius Caesar (100–44 B.C.) responsible for the greatest change in the history of ancient Rome—from a republic to an empire—but he also ordered the calendar that forms the basis for the one we still use today.

The Romans honored Janus, the god of all beginnings and endings (see page 14), by naming a month after him: Januarius (now January).

Ancient peoples found it difficult to work out a calendar, and the Romans were no exception. The early Romans knew that the sun completed a cycle in $365\frac{1}{4}$ days, which they designated a year. They then divided the year into 12 months, based on the appearance in the sky of each new moon.

Besides Januarius, the early Romans named three other months after gods: Martius (March) after Mars; Maius (May) after Maia; and Iunius (June) after Juno. Because Martius came at the start of spring, it was the first month of the calendar year. As for the other months, the early Romans named Februarius (February) after *februs*, a festival of purification. Experts disagree on the naming of Aprilis (April), but it may come from *aperire*, meaning to open, referring to the opening of buds in the spring. The other six months, between Iunius and Januarius, the early Romans simply numbered: Quintilis (the fifth), Sextilis (the sixth), September (the seventh), October (the eighth), November (the ninth), and December (the tenth).

Juno was the goddess for whom the Romans named the month of Iunius (the English June).

New Order

There is a new moon approximately every 29½ days. Twelve cycles of the moon total about 355 days. Therefore the early Romans' 12 months totaled less than a year. By 46 B.C. the Roman calendar was 90 days behind the seasons—Martius was in winter, not spring.

So, on the advice of an astronomer called Sosigenes, Rome's leader, Julius Caesar, decided to reform the calendar. He ordered an extra 90 days to be added to 46 B.C., to bring the calendar into line with the seasons, and decided that future new years would begin with Januarius, to honor Janus. He also added a day or two to some months to bring the number of days in a year to 365. To allow for the extra quarter of a day each year, he ordered an extra day to be added to Februarius every fourth year (now called a leap year).

The Romans called the middle of each month the Ides. In 44 B.C., a fortune-teller warned Caesar to beware the Ides of Martius. On the 15th of Martius, Caesar was assassinated. Quintilis was then renamed Julius (July) in Caesar's honor. Forty years later, Sextilis was changed to Augustus (August) after Caesar's successor, Rome's first emperor.

This is a bust of Julius Caesar, who adopted the system of timekeeping now known as the Julian calendar.

Ceres and Proserpina

When Pluto, the god of the underworld, took Proserpina, the lovely daughter of Ceres, as his wife, the goddess thought she had lost her child forever—until Jupiter intervened.

Ceres (Demeter to the Greeks) was the goddess of fruitfulness. Her brothers were Jupiter (Zeus), the king of the gods, Neptune (Poseidon), the god of the sea, and Pluto (Hades), the god of the underworld.

Ceres had a beautiful daughter, Proserpina (Persephone). To conceal Proserpina from the eyes of the other gods, Ceres took her to Sicily and hid her there. One day, as Proserpina was wandering through the fields, picking flowers, Pluto spied her. He rose up out of the earth in his chariot and carried her off to his kingdom below, where he made her his queen.

When Ceres discovered that her daughter had been kidnapped, she was heartbroken. She left her home on Mount Olympus to search the world for Proserpina and neglected her duties. As a result, the earth was no longer fruitful. Plants withered and died, the animal herds refused to breed, and famine soon stalked the land.

Jupiter learned from Apollo that his brother had taken Proserpina. He tried to persuade Ceres to return to Olympus and so end the famine, but she refused to take up her duties again until her daughter was restored to her.

In desperation, Jupiter ordered Pluto to give up his queen. At first Pluto argued but eventually he agreed that Proserpina could return to the open air. Only then did Jupiter and Ceres discover that Proserpina had eaten pomegranate, the fruit of the dead, at her wedding, meaning that she had made a contract with the underworld forever.

Seasonal Solution

Jupiter then arranged a compromise. Proserpina would spend six months of each year on earth and the other six months in the underworld. From the start of the time Proserpina was to spend with Ceres—spring—plants would burst forth, ripen, and yield fruits and seeds. Then,

when Proserpina returned to the underworld— each fall—the plants would wither and die. Six months later, when Proserpina went back to her mother, they would start to grow again.

Even though she now saw her daughter for only six months each year, Ceres was overjoyed. She gathered sheaves of wheat and gave them to a Greek prince, telling him how to cultivate the grain. In recognition of this, the Greeks worshipped her in secret ceremonies, first held at a town called Eleusis. Other temples to Ceres were built, and many Romans later made long pilgrimages to Greece to worship her at them.

This is a marble statue of the Greek goddess Demeter, who was known to the Romans as Ceres.

Wheat in Ancient Rome

Bread was the staple food of ordinary people in ancient Rome, and the survival of the Roman empire largely depended on a bountiful crop of wheat every year.

So important was wheat to the Romans that they believed it was Ceres, the goddess of fruitfulness, who first taught humans how to cultivate it. The poet Juvenal (around A.D. 60–130) famously wrote that ordinary Romans wanted only two things—bread and circuses. The high price of grain—and a consequent shortage of bread—often sparked riots in the streets of Rome.

The Roman army's rations were based on wheat bread. If soldiers did not reach the required standards in training, their ration was changed from wheat to the less appetizing and cheaper barley until they did.

The free people of the Roman state were known as citizens, but most of them did not live in cities or towns. Instead, they worked the land. As the Romans

This Roman bakery is one of the ruins of Pompeii, which was destroyed in A.D. 79 by an eruption of the volcanic Mount Vesuvius.

Wheat fields were the breadbasket of the Roman empire.

conquered the countries of their neighbors, citizen colonists were given land to cultivate. At first this was sufficient to meet demand but the population of Rome was growing fast. More and more of the land was given over to olive trees, for olive oil, and grape vines, for wine.

When the Romans finally defeated the Carthaginians in 201 B.C. they gained much good grain-growing land in North Africa. For a long time, Sicily and North Africa were the main sources of wheat and barley for the Roman empire. Further supplies were brought in from northern Greece and the Nile River delta in Egypt.

Decline of farming

Rich Romans later began to buy up large farming estates and brought in prisoners of war as slaves to work the land. Soldiers returning from war to their family farms decided that farming was not for them, and went back to their legions. Sometimes they found their farms had already been sold. Families broke up and drifted to Rome, where the emperor had to make free monthly issues of grain to prevent rioting. The gradual disappearance of the farmer-citizens, traditionally the backbone of the army, was one cause of the fall of the Roman empire in the 5th century A.D.

This landscape of olive trees and vineyards is typical of the countryside around the modern city of Florence in Tuscany, central Italy.

The God of Fire

Though crippled from an early age, the fire god Vulcan had massive strength in his arms, which he used to forge metal—and gain revenge on his mother, who cruelly cast him aside.

Vulcan (Hephaestus to the Greeks) was the son of Jupiter (Zeus) and Juno (Hera). Some say that Jupiter and Juno quarreled fiercely one day and that, in her rage, Juno hurled her baby boy off Mount Olympus, the home of the gods. Vulcan fell for nine days and nights, finally landing on the island of Lemnos, twisting his feet and dislocating a hip. Others say he was born crippled, so the gods laughed at him until his mother threw him from the mountain in disgust. He fell into the sea near the island of Naxos.

In either version, Thetis and other nymphs rescued Vulcan and cared for him on Lemnos. Here, hidden in a deep grotto, he learned the secret art of metalworking and planned revenge on his mother. Finally, one day he sent her a beautiful golden throne. Delighted, Juno sat on it right away — and immediately was trapped. All the gods tried to free her, but none succeeded.

Jupiter ordered Vulcan to come and release his mother, but he refused to leave his forge. Vulcan's brother Mars (Ares) tried to drag him out, but he drove him off with fire. Bacchus (Dionysus) had better luck. He got Vulcan to drink too much wine and brought him to Olympus slumped over the back of a mule. Yet Vulcan still refused to free Juno—unless he could marry the beautiful Venus (Aphrodite). Jupiter reluctantly agreed.

Arming the Gods

On Olympus, Vulcan built golden palaces for the gods and a forge where he made thunderbolts for Jupiter, arrows for Cupid (Eros), Diana (Artemis), and Apollo, and armor for many gods and heroes, including Achilles. Vulcan's feeble, lame legs supported his big, strong body with great difficulty, so he constructed two golden female statues that could move and support him when he walked.

Vulcan maintained his old metal works on Lemnos, and kept another forge under Mount Etna, the volcano in Sicily, where he was helped by the giant Cyclopes. Each Cyclops had just one huge eye that glittered menacingly under a single bushy brow.

Vulcan guarded his secret art jealously, until one day Prometheus, son of one of the earliest gods, Oceanus, and a champion of humankind, succeeded in stealing fire from him so that human beings could learn how to forge metal.

Italy has several volcanoes, including Mount Vesuvius near Naples and Mount Etna on the island of Sicily.

Metalwork and Money

Advanced metalwork techniques enabled the ancient Romans to conquer armies that were equipped with inferior weapons and to build a vast empire in which Roman coins were the common currency.

The early Latin farmers did not know how to make metal tools and weapons. They bought them from the Etruscans, who were skilled metalworkers, particularly in gold and bronze, and knew how to extract iron from iron ore. It was not until later that the Romans learned these techniques.

Expertise

Bronze, an alloy of copper and tin, was easily melted in furnaces at about 900°F (480°C), so that it could be cast in a mold. Iron was difficult to extract from its ore, which had to be heated to around 3,000°F (1,600°C). At this temperature, the ore formed a spongy lump, which was hammered to drive out the waste products. The lump was then reheated and shaped into a tool or a weapon, which was "case-hardened" by thrusting it into glowing charcoal.

The quality of weapons made in this way was shown when the Romans defeated the Gauls at the Battle of Addua in Italy in 223 B.C. The historian Polybius contrasted the mighty Roman swords with those of the enemy, which were "easily bent, and gave only one downward cut."

> In A.D. 145, the Emperor Marcus Aurelius issued coins bearing his own image.

ROMAN COINS

When the Romans first started issuing money, the principal coin was an *as*, a lump of bronze weighing nearly one pound (2.2 kg). Twelve smaller coins, called *uncia*, or ounces, made up one *as*. In time, as the *as* lost its value, the Romans introduced other coins, including the alloy sestertius, the silver denarius, and the gold aureus. Initially, coins had images of Rome, animals, gods, or scenes from mythology stamped on one side, but after the republic became an empire, in 27 B.C., they had images of the emperor stamped on them.

Swords such as this were the standard issue to Roman legionaries during the imperial age.

Early Money

For several hundred years after the founding of Rome, Greece remained the leading power in the eastern Mediterranean. Greek ships brought a wide range of trade goods to Rome, tying up at the mouth of the Tiber River. At first, the Romans paid for these goods with grain and cattle, but the Greek merchants paid for the products they purchased with copper and silver coins. Gradually the Romans began to use money themselves in the form of rough lumps of bronze that could be almost any shape or weight. They did not issue their first coins until around 350 B.C.

Apollo and Daphne

When a lovely maiden chose to be turned into a laurel tree rather than have her purity defiled by Apollo, the god designated a laurel wreath as the highest mark of honor.

One day, the god Apollo had a quarrel with Cupid (Eros to the Greeks) over which of them was the greater archer. Apollo scorned the power of Cupid's arrows, saying it was impossible that they could make someone fall in love with anyone Cupid chose, because Cupid was so young and small. In revenge for this grievous insult, Cupid had Vulcan (Hephaestus), the god of fire, fashion him two arrows—one sharp and tipped with gold, the other blunt and tipped with lead—and fired them into the air. The gold-tipped arrow struck Apollo, immediately causing him to fall desperately in love with a beautiful mountain nymph called Daphne. The lead-tipped arrow struck Daphne, causing her to reject all declarations of love.

Apollo had a rival in Leucippus, a mortal who was also in love with Daphne. The daughter of Mother Earth, Gaea, and the Peneus River in Thessaly (a region of Greece), Daphne was a priestess. She and other nymphs devoted to Gaea performed secret rites that were forbidden to men. Leucippus decided to disguise himself as a woman so that he could follow the nymphs, discover the rites that they performed, and make himself known to Daphne. Dressed as a woman, he soon gained Daphne's confidence. When Apollo found out what Leucippus was doing, he cunningly suggested to the nymphs that they make bathing naked an essential part of their ceremonies, so that everything about their rituals would be pure and undefiled. In doing so, the nymphs discovered that Leucippus was a man, and in fury they tore him to pieces.

Transformation

Now the field of love was open to Apollo—or so he believed. He found a way to approach Daphne and declared his passion for her. When she rejected him outright, he tried to grab her, but she slipped out of his grasp and ran away. Apollo gave chase and gained on Daphne, who became more and more terrified. Eventually she came to the bank of a river. There, with nowhere left to run, she called on her mother, Gaea, to save her. The next moment, as Daphne stood on the riverbank shaking with fright, she felt her feet becoming rooted into the ground. Then her flesh began to turn into bark and her arms stretched out in the form of long branches, with her hands and fingers becoming glossy green leaves.

By the time Apollo caught up with Daphne and threw his arms around her, he found himself embracing not his true love but a laurel tree. The god realized then that he lost the nymph forever. To console himself, he made a wreath of laurel leaves for his head, declaring that, from that moment onward, the laurel was his sacred tree and its leaves the greatest symbol of honor.

These two sculptures show the god Apollo (right) chasing the nymph Daphne (left).

The Romans in Battle

By conquering foreign lands, Rome was able to safeguard and feed its ever-growing population, so generals who led Roman armies to victory were hailed as heroes by their emperor.

When Apollo tried to embrace the nymph Daphne, she turned into a laurel tree, which the god then declared a symbol of honor. A laurel wreath thus became the highest mark of glory. In Rome, when a general returned in triumph, the whole city celebrated, and the emperor placed a laurel wreath on the victor's head.

Growing Army

The Romans began to expand their boundaries soon after the founding of Rome in about 750 B.C. Much of the land they conquered was given to farmers on condition they served as soldiers whenever needed. Later, other citizens were drawn into the part-time army with the promise of pay. The Roman army was organized in this way until around 100 B.C., when semiprofessional volunteers began to strengthen it. Eventually the Roman army became fully professional, with soldiers on 20-year contracts.

Most soldiers were infantrymen called legionaries. The smallest unit was the *contubernium*—eight men who shared a tent and a pack mule. Ten of these units made up a century, which was led by a

Roman military triumphs were commemorated by carvings on Trajan's Column in Rome.

centurion. Six centuries made a cohort, and ten cohorts a legion of almost 5,000 men. Each legion also had a few hundred specialist troops, including archers and cavalrymen.

One reason for the Roman army's success was its superior weaponry. At the start of a

Legionaries sometimes formed a *testudo*, or tortoise, advancing close together with shields interlocked on all sides and overhead.

This is a typical soldier of the Roman legions.

battle, each legionary threw a *pilum*, or javelin with an untempered metal shaft that bent on impact, making it difficult to pull out and impossible to hurl back. Hand to hand, a legionary fought with a *gladius*, a 20-inch (50-cm), pointed, two-edged stabbing sword.

Every legion also had specialist engineers who built wooden bridges, siege towers, battering rams, and *ballistae* (catapults that hurled rocks) to attack forts and walled cities.

Bloodthirsty Mars

Early in Roman history, Mars was a god of farming as well as of war. Then the Romans identified him with the ferociously bloodthirsty Greek god Ares, who was exclusively a god of war.

Some stories say that Mars (Ares) was the son of Jupiter (Zeus) and Juno (Hera), king and queen of the Olympian gods, others that he was born from the union of Juno with a magical herb brought to her by Flora, the goddess of flowers and spring. Either way, Mars grew up to become the god of war.

Tall and handsome, cruel and vain, Mars liked nothing better than to shed the blood of his opponents in the midst of a fierce battle. Whenever he heard the clash of weapons and yells of war, Mars donned his gleaming helmet, leaped onto his chariot, and gleefully rode into the thick of the fray. Drawn by two fast horses called Fear and Panic, the bloodthirsty god raged about the battlefield, cutting down men with his great sword. Sometimes he slaughtered men on both sides, not caring in the least who won and who lost, so long as he wreaked maximum carnage and spilled as much blood as he could.

The other gods disliked Mars because of his constant thirst for violence, so when he killed one of the many sons of Neptune (Poseidon), the god of the sea, they saw it as the ideal opportunity to punish him. Summoning Mars, the gods put him on trial for murder but when Mars's daughter testified that her father had killed Neptune's son because the boy had attacked her, the disappointed gods had no choice but to let Mars go.

The Trojan Wars

In spite of Mars's great strength, other gods and heroes often beat him in combat. During the siege of Troy Mars fought on the side of the Trojans, while the goddess of war and wisdom, Minerva (Athena), supported the Greeks. Mars was furious when he caught sight of her and struck out at her shield. Minerva drew back and felled Mars with a huge stone, saying, "Fool! Haven't you yet learned how my strength is greater than yours?"

This is a statue of Ares, the ancient Greek god of war, who became Mars in Roman mythology.

Later, when Mars challenged the mighty Hercules (Heracles), the great hero wounded Mars and he stumbled, groaning, back to Mount Olympus, the home of the gods. On another occasion, two giants, Otus and Ephialtis, other sons of Neptune, managed to capture Mars and bind him in iron. He was their prisoner for 13 months, until Mercury (Hermes), the messenger of the gods, stealthily released him.

Mars constantly fell in love. His most famous affair was with Venus (Aphrodite), the goddess of love, but he had many other relationships and many children, including Romulus, the founder of Rome.

During the reign of Numa Pompilius, who succeeded Romulus as ruler of Rome, Mars let a shield fall from the sky. The Romans believed this was a sign that they had the protection of the god. To ensure that no one would steal the shield, Numa Pompilius had 11 copies made. These were kept under guard in the Temple of Vesta (Hestia), the goddess of the hearth, in the Forum in Rome.

Bloodshed in the Arena

Rome built its empire on bloody conquest. To show their power, emperors held brutal public games in huge arenas called amphitheaters, fueling the bloodlust of the people.

This photograph shows the interior of the Colosseum in Rome as it appears today. It was once the greatest stadium of the empire.

The Romans celebrated the god of war and courage, Mars (Ares to the Greeks), for his bloodthirstiness. Across the empire, in dozens of amphitheaters, they held frequent games in which people and animals savagely butchered each other.

The biggest amphitheater was the Colosseum in Rome. Completed in A.D. 80, it held 50,000 spectators, all baying for blood. Emperors held free games here on public holidays. To outdo their predecessors, succeeding emperors held bigger and bloodier games. The carnage reached its peak in A.D. 107, when the Emperor Trajan presided over the deaths of 10,000 people and as many animals in 120 days of slaughter.

Killing Schedule

A typical day's killing began mid-morning with games called *venationes*. Animals such as lions, bears, leopards, elephants, and ostriches were let loose on each other, on criminals, and on prisoners of war—men, women, and children—and were then massacred by trained men called *bestiarii*.

> **This fragment of a marble frieze shows two ancient Roman gladiators, one armed with a trident, the other with a sword.**

Some prisoners were forced to fight each other to the death—man against man, woman against woman, child against child.

At midday the mangled and mutilated bodies were removed. Perfume was sprinkled on the wealthy spectators in the front rows to mask the stench of guts, and fresh sand was spread over the bloody floor.

To a fanfare of horns, trained gladiators—mainly specially chosen prisoners of war, but also a few thrill-seeking citizens—then entered the arena, called out to the emperor, "We who are about to die salute you!" and drew lots to form pairs that fought one another to the death.

CHARIOT RACING

Another bloody spectacle Romans bet on was chariot racing. The biggest arena was Rome's Circus Maximus, which held 250,000 people. Four to twelve chariots from four imperial teams—Reds, Whites, Blues, and Greens—raced seven times around the *spina*, or central barrier, a distance of 5 miles (8 km). There might be two dozen races in a day. The charioteers were trained slaves who raced for gold. The best might buy their freedom, but many died in collisions, when forced into the wall, or when overturning on the tight curves.

Mars and Venus

When Mars and Venus became lovers on Mount Olympus, the home of the gods, they thought their secret was safe—not reckoning on the cunning of Venus's husband, Vulcan.

Born from the foam of the sea, the extraordinarily beautiful goddess of love, Venus (Aphrodite to the Greeks), wore a magic belt that made everyone who saw her fall in love with her. On the orders of Jupiter (Zeus), the king of the gods, she married the god of fire, Vulcan (Hephaestus), who alone knew the secret art of metalworking. Unfortunately, Vulcan was ugly and lame in one leg, and Venus soon found a more exciting lover in his brother Mars (Ares), the god of war and courage. She bore Mars three children, including Cupid (Eros), without Vulcan suspecting that they were not his own.

Mars ordered his faithful servant Alectryon to keep watch each night so that no one would discover him and Venus together, but early one morning Alectryon fell asleep at his post. As a result, the lovers stayed too long together and were caught by the rays of the rising sun, which belonged to Apollo. Mars was so furious at this that he immediately turned Alectryon into a rooster, to remind him that it was his job to give warning of the approaching dawn.

Vulcan soon learned from Apollo of his wife's deception and planned his revenge. Working secretly in his sweltering forge he made a marvelous net of bronze—a net so fine that it was invisible, yet so strong that it was unbreakable.

Vulcan hung the net over his wife's bed and told her he was setting out on a journey to the island of Lemnos, where he was raised as a boy and had another forge. Venus and Mars thought this was an ideal chance to be together. At dawn the next day they awoke to find themselves entangled in the net.

Dragnet

Vulcan, of course, had only pretended to go to Lemnos. On finding the two lovers trapped, he gathered them up in the net like fish and hauled them before the other gods for them to laugh at. The gods duly

This fresco on a wall in the House of Venus in Pompeii shows the goddess Venus with attendant nymphs.

roared with laughter at the sight of Mars and Venus, naked and embarrassed, in the net. Apollo nudged Mercury (Hermes), the messenger of the gods, and asked him if he would willingly take the place of Mars inside the net. Mercury swore that he would, but Jupiter, disgusted by the whole situation, refused to allow any interference in a quarrel between a husband and his wife. In the end, Neptune (Poseidon), the god of the sea, secured the release of Mars by undertaking that Mars would pay a fee to Vulcan equal to the value of Venus's wedding gifts. "And if he doesn't," said Neptune, "then I myself will pay, and marry Venus!"

Later, as a punishment, Jupiter made Venus fall in love with Anchises, a prince of Troy. She gave birth to a son, who was Aeneas, the ancestor of the Roman people.

Family Life

Parents in ancient Rome had complete control over the lives of their offspring, arranging their marriages so that they would produce children of their own and so carry on the family line.

The *familia*, or family, was all-important to the Romans, who honored their ancestors and saw it as a duty to marry and have children.

At the head of the family was the paterfamilias, who wielded *potestas*, or power, over his wife and children. Boys usually married between the ages of 15 and 18, girls married as young as 13. Parents chose their children's partners from families of equal standing.

For Richer, For Poorer

There was no standard wedding ceremony, nor were there any legally binding vows. In poor families, the girl might simply move in with the boy. There was usually a written contract, though, by which the girl passed from the *manus*, or guardianship, of her father into the care of the boy, and the girl's family gave the boy's family a dowry.

In wealthy families, on the day of the wedding, the girl gave up her toys and childhood toga, had her

This is a Roman sculpture of a mother (left) and her baby (right).

hair done, put on special clothes, and waited at home. When the boy and his family arrived, a pig was sacrificed, and the couple exchanged vows. After the families had shared breakfast and swapped gifts, the boy symbolically dragged the girl from her mother's arms, and everyone set out for his house. Some guests carried torches lit from the girl's hearth, others threw walnuts as symbols of fertility. The girl carried a spindle, symbolizing her new role as a wife.

The boy went on ahead to greet the girl's arrival. When she arrived, the torches were thrown away, and the girl symbolically rubbed the doorway with oil and wreathed it with wool. Because it was considered unlucky for her to trip on entering the boy's home, he often carried her over the threshold.

CHILDREN AND SCHOOLING

Poor Roman children helped their parents at work as soon as they were able to and seldom learned to read or write. In most wealthy families, girls learned only household skills, from their mothers. Education was for boys, who from the age of 7 learned Latin, Greek, and arithmetic at a private school, from sunrise to noon, five days a week. Learning was by rote, and pupils were beaten for failing. From the age of 11 they also learned history, literature, and philosophy. Educated slaves called pedagogues, who were usually Greek, sometimes taught the boys at home. In rich families, boys learned the art of public speaking in preparation for careers in law or politics.

The Messenger of the Gods

A cunning trickster, Mercury made mischief from the moment he was born. He so delighted his father, Jupiter, the king of the gods, that Jupiter made him the gods' messenger.

Mercury (Hermes to the Greeks), son of Jupiter (Zeus) and Maia, a goddess of nature, was born in a cave on Mount Cyllene in Arcadia, a region of Greece. Maia wrapped the baby boy in swaddling clothes, but he wriggled free while she slept and fled to Thessaly, where his brother, Apollo, grazed cattle. Mercury stole the herd, drove it home—making the cows walk backward and wearing his shoes back to front, so Apollo would not know where they had gone—and hid it in a grotto. Then he killed a tortoise and one of the cows and made a lyre, using the shell of the tortoise as the sound box and the gut of the cow for strings. He then sneaked back into the cave and wrapped himself in his swaddling clothes again.

An old man saw what Mercury had done and told Apollo, who dragged the mischievous baby off to Mount Olympus, the home of the gods, and complained to their father. Jupiter was greatly amused at the tricks of his baby son, but Apollo remained angry until Mercury enchanted him by playing sweet music on his lyre. Mercury then tactfully offered his brother the instrument in exchange for the herd, and Apollo happily agreed. Jupiter was so delighted with Mercury's diplomacy that he made him messenger of the gods, guardian of roads, and protector of travelers, and gave him winged sandals.

Divine Musician

Although he had given Apollo his lyre, Mercury still loved music, and one of his own sons, the goat-god Faunus, taught him to make and play reed pipes while he watched over his herd. He also made a

flute, which Apollo greatly admired, so he swapped it for the caduceus, or golden staff, that Apollo always carried. For hundreds of years on earth, heralds—the diplomatic messengers of kings and emperors—carried a staff to show they were under divine protection. Mercury's uncle, Pluto (Hades), god of the underworld, would send for him to lay his staff on the eyes of the dying so that they would travel peacefully to the underworld.

As well as being guardian of roads and protector of travelers, Mercury came to represent all kinds of communication and quick-witted ideas, and he was the god of merchants and trade. To honor him, people erected stones along the roads where traders traveled. Later, these became the milestones of more modern times.

This beautiful figurine represents Mercury, the winged messenger of the gods, standing on top of the world.

Music in Ancient Rome

Together with dancing, music was a popular form of light entertainment in ancient Rome. It also played an important role in religious ceremonies and at public spectacles, such as chariot races and the games at the Colosseum.

The Romans regarded music not as serious art to be appreciated, but as something simply to be enjoyed. This is evident from the story of Mercury (Hermes to the Greeks), the fun-loving messenger of the gods who enjoyed playing the lyre and panpipes, both of which were popular in ancient Rome.

Like many Roman instruments, the lyre, or kithara, was Greek in origin. The player plucked its strings like a harp, and its box amplified the sound like an acoustic guitar.

Simple wind instruments such as panpipes were probably the most common kind played in ancient Rome. The traditional instrument of shepherds, panpipes were made from reed or cane whistles of different lengths: the shorter the whistle, the higher the note. They were played like a harmonica, or mouth organ. Another popular wind instrument was the bone tibia, or pipe, with three or four finger holes to vary the note. Some musicians even played double pipes—a pair of boxwood, ivory, or silver pipes, one for each hand, that were blown at the same time.

The most complicated wind instrument, if not the most portable one, was the water organ, which was invented in Greece in the third century B.C. A pump forced water into a closed chamber to

In Greek and Roman mythology, every form of art had its own goddess, known as a Muse. This is Euterpe, the Muse of music.

compress the air inside, then hand-operated valves released bursts of air through pipes of varying size to produce different notes, like the bellows of a modern organ.

Strolling players

Like street musicians today, small bands of men sang and played for money in the streets of Rome, often accompanied by female dancers clicking castanets. Wealthy Romans, meanwhile, often hired professional musicians called virtuosi, who were often Greek, to entertain themselves and their guests between the many courses at lavish dinner parties. Many virtuosi also held concerts and performed in plays at outdoor theaters.

This mosaic shows musicians and gladiators performing at a Roman circus in the colony of Leptis Magna (modern Libya).

Music and dance were also important parts of worship in some of the many Eastern "mystery" cults that became popular in ancient Rome. The cults popularized instruments such as the sistrum, a metal rattle played by devotees of the Egyptian goddess Isis.

Loud instruments were also played at the biggest outdoor events—the chariot races at the Circus Maximus and the gladiatorial games in the arena of the Colosseum. They included tambourines, metal cymbals, and straight bronze horns.

The God of Revelry

Bacchus, a son of Jupiter, king of the gods, grew up far from his Mediterranean home but eventually returned in triumph, teaching people the secret art of winemaking and gathering an army of faithful followers.

Harmonia, a daughter of the god of war, Mars (Ares to the Greeks), and his lover, the goddess Venus (Aphrodite), married Cadmus, founder of Thebes, and bore him four children. Their youngest daughter, Semele, became a lover of Jupiter (Zeus). Jupiter's wife, Juno (Hera), was jealous of Semele and, disguised as her old nurse, persuaded her to beg Jupiter to visit her in his godly rather than his human form. Jupiter duly arrived surrounded by thunderbolts and lightning, which burned Semele to death.

Semele was pregnant at the time of her death, but Mercury (Hermes), the messenger of the gods, saved her unborn son from the flames. Jupiter then hid him until it was time for him to be born. The boy was Bacchus (Dionysus). To protect Bacchus from Juno, Jupiter placed him in the care of Silenus, a son of the goat-god Faunus, on Mount Nysa in faraway India.

Silenus brought Bacchus up, educated him, and became his faithful follower.

Bacchus happily roamed the mountains and forests, an ivy wreath around his head, and learned from Silenus the secret art of turning grapes into wine.

The young Bacchus then decided to return to Greece. On his long journey he led an army of women and men, all playing musical instruments, and rode in a chariot pulled by a lion and a tiger. Everywhere he went, people welcomed him, because he taught them how to make wine. Very soon people worshipped him as the god of wine and revelry, and his female followers, called bacchantes, celebrated wild, drunken parties.

Homecoming

When Bacchus reached the Greek islands, pirates kidnapped him, thinking he was a king's son and hoping for a ransom. They tried to tie him with ropes, but the knots instantly came loose. Then the sea around their ship turned into rich wine, a vine sprouted from the mast and tangled the sail, and ivy wound itself round the mast. Finally, Bacchus turned himself into a fierce lion. The terrified pirates leapt into the sea, where they at once turned into dolphins.

Arriving safely on the island of Naxos, Bacchus found Ariadne, daughter of the king of Crete, dumped there by the hero Theseus. On seeing Bacchus she burst into tears, but he soon cheered her up, and they married shortly afterward.

This ancient Roman mosaic shows Bacchus with a headdress made of vine leaves and grapes.

Food and Drink

The Romans are famous for eating and drinking to excess, but only the wealthy few could ever afford to overindulge. Most people in ancient Rome lived on a frugal daily diet.

The image of potbellied Romans lounging drunkenly on couches, holding out goblets for slaves to refill, is a familiar one, but even occasional bingeing on food and wine was a luxury that only the rich could afford.

This photograph shows the ornately decorated interior of a house in Herculaneum, the Roman town that was destroyed, with Pompeii, by an eruption of Mount Vesuvius in A.D. 79.

Daily Diet

Typically, Romans ate a light breakfast of bread and cheese at dawn and a small lunch at noon. For the wealthy, lunch might be a little fish or meat, with a few olives, grapes, or figs. Their main meal was dinner, begun in the afternoon and timed to end before sunset.

For the well-to-do, dinner was leisurely, and sometimes lavish. Dancers, clowns, jugglers, acrobats, musicians, and poets might entertain guests in between the three to ten courses of the meal. Diners dressed in elegant Greek robes called syntheses and reclined on couches around low tables to which slaves brought in food and wine and fingerbowls, for Romans ate with the fingers of their right hand.

The first course might be olives, peahens' eggs, salad, and shellfish such as oysters. Main courses featured meat such as venison, wild boar, hare, and snails, fish such as sturgeon, and poultry—anything from chicken and goose to flamingo, ostrich, and peacock.

Roman cooks—trained slaves—prided themselves on serving exotic dishes. One recipe was for dormice in honey and poppyseeds, while another was for quails and quails' eggs with asparagus. Transportation was slow, so meat, fish, and poultry were rarely fresh. To disguise their taste, rich sauces, herbs, and spices all featured strongly in the dishes. Expensive spices came from Asia, while a highly prized sauce made from sun-dried, salted fish guts came from southern Spain.

Dinner ended with a dessert of fruit, dates, nuts, and honey cakes. These were washed down, like each course, with wines, which were diluted with water.

This Roman mosaic shows two men treading grapes at the start of the winemaking process.

Glossary

Actaeon A hunter who was turned into a stag by Diana.

Aeneas Prince of Troy, son of Venus, and ancestor of Romulus. He is the central character in Virgil's *Aeneid*.

Alba Longa Ancient Latin village out of which grew Rome.

Apollo God of sunlight, music, healing, and prophecy.

as Ancient Roman coin weighing nearly 1 lb (0.5 kg).

Ascanius Son of Aeneas and founder of Alba Longa.

augurs Special priests who were consulted by politicians and rulers to read the future and predict the outcome of a decision.

aureus An ancient Roman coin made of gold, originally equal to 25 silver denarii (see denarius).

Bacchus God of wine.

caduceus Apollo's golden staff, which he traded to Mercury for a special flute.

Carthaginians (Carthage) North African civilization that ruled much of the western Mediterranean, including parts of Italy. For many years, they were Rome's main rival.

centurion An officer commanding a century (around 80 soldiers).

Ceres Goddess of agriculture and sister of Jupiter.

Circus Maximus Rome's largest arena for chariot racing.

Colosseum Ancient Rome's largest amphitheater, capacity 50,000.

Cupid God of love.

Daphne A beautiful nymph who was loved by Apollo but turned into a laurel tree to escape him.

denarius A Roman coin made of silver, worth 10 bronze *asses* (see *as*).

Diana Goddess of wild animals and the hunt.

Etruscans (Etruria) Pre-Roman civilization that ruled much of Italy for 250 years. In the fifth century B.C., they began to lose power to Rome.

Faunus A woodland god, appearing half man, half goat.

Flora Goddess of flowers.

Forum Site of Rome's main market and judicial buildings.

gladius A 20-inch (50-cm), two-edged stabbing sword used by Roman soldiers in battle.

Heracles Mythical hero of superhuman strength.

Janus A major Roman god with two faces. Guardian of doors, gates, and beginnings.

Juno Queen of the gods and wife of Jupiter.

Jupiter King of the gods.

kithara A large lyre, Greek in origin, with a resonating box.

lararium A shrine in the home dedicated to a specific god.

lares Small statue of a god placed in a *lararium*.

laurel wreath Symbol of honor worn by victorious generals during processions through Rome.

lyre A musical instrument similar to a small harp.

Mars God of war.

Mercury Messenger of the gods.

Minerva Goddess of war.

Neptune God of the sea and brother of Jupiter.

Numa Pompilius Succeeded Romulus as leader of Rome and received a shield from Mars.

nymphs Beautiful female nature spirits of forests and mountains.

Palatine Hill on which Romulus first built Rome.

panpipes A wind instrument made from reed or cane whistles of different lengths.

paterfamilias Male head of a Roman family.

pedagogue Usually a well-educated Greek slave who taught his master's sons in their home.

Pluto God of the underworld and brother of Jupiter.

Proserpina Daughter of Ceres and wife of Pluto.

rex silvae ("king of the woods") The priest at Nemi, a special shrine to the goddess Diana.

Romulus Brother of Remus and mythical founder of Rome.

Saturn Father of Jupiter and most other major gods.

sestertius An ancient Roman coin made of alloy, originally worth 2½ bronze *asses* (see *as*).

tibia A wind instrument made of hollowed bone with three or four holes to make different notes. It was played like a recorder or clarinet.

Trojans Ancient civilization said by the Romans to be their ancestors. Their destruction is depicted in Homer's *Iliad* and Virgil's *Aeneid*.

uncia Small Roman coins worth one-twelfth of an *as*.

Venus Goddess of love.

Vestal Virgin A virgin dedicated to Vesta, goddess of the hearth.

Virgil Born in 70 B.C. and died in 19 B.C., poet and author of the *Aeneid*, which gives a mythological explanation of the origin of Rome.

virtuosi Professional musicians who performed at dinner parties.

viscera Entrails or internal organs from a sacrificed animal that were studied by priests attempting to read the future from them.

Vulcan God of fire and volcanoes, and blacksmith to the other gods.

Further Information

BOOKS

Allan, Tony. *The Roman World*. Mankato, MN: Zak Books, 2009.

Boatwright, Mary T., Daniel J. Gargola, and Richard J. A. Talbert. *The Romans: From Village to Empire*. New York, NY: Oxford University Press, 2004.

Defrasne, Jean (translated by Barbara Whelpton). *Stories from Roman History*. Cleveland, IL: World, 1965.

James, Simon, et al. *Eyewitness: Ancient Rome*. New York, NY: Dorling Kindersley, 2000.

McCaughrean, Geraldine. *Roman Myths*. New York, NY: Margaret McElderry Books, 2001.

Paige, Joy. *Roman Mythology*. New York, NY: Rosen, 2006.

Scurman, Ike. *Ancient Roman Civilization*. New York, NY: Rosen, 2010.

Stroud, Jonathan. *Sightseers: Ancient Rome*. New York, NY: Larousse Kingfisher Chambers, 2000.

VIDEOS

Ancient Rome: The Glorious Empire. Kultur Video, 1999.

Ancient Rome: Story of an Empire. Arts & Entertainment Video, 1998.

Great Cities of the Ancient World: Rome and Pompeii. Questar Incorporated, 1993.

Just the Facts: Ancient Rome. Goldhil Home Media, 2001.

WEB SITES

Ancient Rome: The History of Ancient Rome
http://ancienthistory.about.com/od/romeancientrome/

A History of Ancient Rome
http://www.historylearningsite.co.uk/a_history_of_ancient_rome.htm

Kidipede
http://www.historyforkids.org/learn/romans

Roman Gods
http://gwydir.demon.co.uk/jo/roman/index.htm

Index